IS-545: Reconstitution Planning Course

By

Fema

8/11/2014

Lesson 1 — Introduction and Course Overview

Overview

Welcome to the Federal Emergency Management Agency's (FEMA's) Reconstitution Planning course.

The purpose of this course is to identify and explore the requirements needed to build and execute a comprehensive reconstitution plan, and to provide you with the knowledge and tools to outline and create or refine a reconstitution plan that will meet the needs of your organization.

Screen Features

The screen features for this course include:

- Click on the **Exit** button to close this window and access the menu listing all lessons of this course. You can select any of the lessons from this menu by simply clicking on the lesson title.
- Click on the **Glossary** button to look up key definitions and acronyms.
- Click on the **Help** button to review guidance and troubleshooting advice regarding navigating through the course.
- Track your progress by looking at the **Progress** bar at the top right of each screen. To see a numeric display, roll your mouse over the Progress bar area.
- Follow the bolded green instructions that appear on each screen in order to proceed to the next screen or complete a Knowledge Check or exercise.
- Click on the **Back** or the **Next** buttons at the top and bottom of screens to move backward or forward in the lesson. **Note**: If the **Next** button is **dimmed**, you must complete an activity before you can proceed in the lesson.

Navigating Using Your Keyboard

Below are instructions for navigating through the course using your keyboard.

- Use the "Tab" key to move forward through each screen's navigation buttons and hyperlinks, or "Shift" + "Tab" to move backwards. A box surrounds the button that is currently selected. 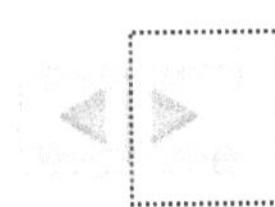

- Press "Enter" to select a navigation button or hyperlink.

- Use the arrow keys to select answers for multiple-choice review questions or self-assessment checklists. Then tab to the "Submit" button and press "Enter" to complete a Knowledge Check or Self-Assessment. 

- **Warning:** Repeatedly pressing "Tab" beyond the number of selections on the screen may cause the keyboard to lock up. Use "Ctrl" + "Tab" to deselect an element or reset to the beginning of a screen's navigation links (most often needed for screens with animations or media).

- JAWS assistive technology users can press the Ctrl key to quiet the screen reader while the course audio plays.

Receiving Credit

To receive credit for this course, you must:

- **Complete all of the lessons.** Each lesson will take between 15 and 35 minutes to complete. It is important to allow enough time to complete the course in its entirety. Check the length of the lesson on the overview screen. Remember, **YOU MUST COMPLETE THE ENTIRE COURSE TO RECEIVE CREDIT.** If you have to leave the course, do not exit from the course or close your browser. If you exit from the course, you will need to start that lesson over again.

- **Pass the final exam.** The last screen provides instructions on how to complete the final exam.

Course Structure

This course is designed to allow you to proceed at your own pace. You will be presented a total of seven lessons, including this course overview:

- Lesson 1: Introduction and Course Overview
- Lesson 2: Reconstitution Requirements
- Lesson 3: Types of Reconstitution
- Lesson 4: Reconstitution Teams
- Lesson 5: Elements of Reconstitution
- Lesson 6: Building a Reconstitution Plan
- Lesson 7: Course Summary

Purpose

This course was created to help you:

- Develop an effective and comprehensive understanding of:
    - Reconstitution requirements.
    - The different types of reconstitution planning.
    - Reconstitution planning teams.
    - Special considerations for reconstitution.
- Begin to develop a reconstitution plan or update and improve an existing plan.

Note: As you proceed through this course, you may find it helpful to create your own separate list of "take-aways" for further consideration as you work to build or improve your organization's reconstitution plan.

Continuity Basics — A Review

Continuity provides clarity regarding expectations and is:

- A good business practice.
- An obligation to constituents.
- A collective understanding of leadership priorities.

Examples of continuity situations include:

- Superstorm Sandy
- Hurricane Katrina
- September 11
- Anthrax attacks
- Flooding
- Wildfires
- Cyber attack

National Continuity Policy

You need to be familiar with the National Continuity Policy, also referred to as National Security Presidential Directive-51/Homeland Security Presidential Directive-20 (NSPD-51/HSPD-20). This Federal policy states:

It is the policy of the United States to maintain a comprehensive and effective continuity capability composed of continuity of operations and continuity of Government programs in order to ensure the preservation of our form of government under the Constitution and the continuing performance of National Essential Functions under all conditions.

This is a Federal policy, however, the idea of continuity is just as important at the State and local levels too!

In this course we will present Federal policies and requirements. With this in mind, some aspects of Federal policies do not apply to State and local organizations. Nevertheless, State and local organizations are encouraged to adopt those practices and recommendations that make sense for their situation and to modify those practices that require adjustment.

Note: Some States and local governments have their own established continuity policies.

Four Operational Phases of Continuity

The four operational phases of continuity include:

1. Readiness and preparedness:
    - Planning
    - Test, training, and exercises
2. Activation and relocation:
    - Communications
    - Transitions
3. Continuity operations:
    - Accounting for personnel
    - Performing essential functions
4. Reconstitution:
    - Returning to full and normal operations

Note: During activation and relocation, some essential functions may have to be accomplished.

Readiness and Preparedness Phase

- Readiness is the ability of an organization to respond to a continuity situation.
- Readiness is a function of planning and training.
    - It is the responsibility of an agency's leadership to ensure that the organization — through normal procedures and with a continuity plan — can perform its essential functions before, during, and after all-hazards emergencies or disasters.

- This phase includes development, review, and revision of plans; Tests, Training, and Exercises (TT&E); risk management; and other preparedness activities.

It is important that you coordinate with partners during the planning phase to ensure that during a disruption that affects the region where an organization operates, the support you require from others (partners) to perform your essential functions will be available.

Activation and Relocation Phase

Agencies must attain an operational continuity capability as soon as possible and with minimal disruption to essential operations, but in all cases within 12 hours of activation.

The activation and relocation includes the following activities:

- The occurrence of an event or the threat of an event
- The decision to activate continuity plans
- Alerting all staff including continuity personnel
- Relocation to alternate or other continuity facilities
- Continued performance of Mission Essential Functions (MEFs)
- Ensuring complete accountability of continuity personnel
- Identification of required and available leadership
- Submitting of Continuity Status Report (CSR)

Continuity Operations Phase

This phase includes the following activities to continue, and ensures performance of essential functions:

- Accounting for all agency personnel
- Establishing communications with supporting and supported agencies, customers, and stakeholders
- Performing essential functions (which may depend on the situation)
- Preparing for reconstitution of the organization

Reconstitution Phase

Reconstitution will not begin until the crisis or threat is over — thus, reconstitution will occur on a "good day." This is important to recognize, since the crisis mentality that drove activation and relocation should no longer exist. Reconstitution should be conducted in a calm, planned, methodical manner.

The following are important things to note about the reconstitution phase:

- Reconstitution is normally conducted using a priority-based approach.

- As an organization continues the performance of essential functions, those functions that were deferred or discontinued because of the emergency must be reconstituted.
- All personnel should be informed that the crisis no longer exists and normal operations are (or will be) resuming.
- Instructions for resumption of normal operations are provided, including supervising an orderly return to the original operating facility, moving to a temporary facility, or moving to a new permanent facility.
- Organizations should begin to develop an after action report/implementation plan (AAR/IP) and track results in the corrective action program (CAP).

Remember, reconstitution is **NOT** conducted in crisis mode.

Continuity Elements

There are ten elements of continuity:

1. **Essential Functions**
2. Orders of Succession
3. Delegations of Authority
4. Continuity Facilities
5. Continuity Communications
6. **Essential Records**
7. **Human Capital**
8. **Tests, Training, and Exercises**
9. Devolution
10. **Reconstitution**

Each of these elements will have to be considered as part of reconstitution. For the purposes of this course, however, the items listed in bold will be covered in more detail.

Note: All of these elements are addressed in the Continuity Manager and Planners courses.

Essential Functions

Essential functions are a subset of all Government functions. Government functions can be defined simply as all of the things the Government does. Essential functions, however, are those activities an organization determines cannot be deferred during an emergency.

These activities must be performed continuously or resumed quickly following a disruption.

Essential functions serve as key continuity planning factors necessary to determine appropriate staffing, communications, essential records, facilities, training, and other requirements.

Essential means important and urgent!

Essential Functions (continued)

Categories of essential functions include:

- MEFs — are those essential functions that directly provide the goods and services the organization was established to produce. Generally, MEFs are UNIQUE to the organization — no one else performs those functions.
- Essential Supporting Activities (ESAs) — are those essential functions that support the organization's performance of their MEFs. Typically ESAs are common to most agencies (e.g., paying staff or providing a secure workplace), but do not accomplish the agency's mission.
- Actions to preserve or protect people, records, equipment, facilities, and capabilities — Protecting and preserving resources is an essential function. Even though many functions can be deferred (and thus the resources to perform them may not be required during the continuity activation), these resources must be available to enable full restoration of activities to occur. If an organization's people, equipment, facilities, and records are not protected, the organization will not be able to reconstitute.
- Reconstitution and long-term recovery activities — Reconstitution involves those essential functions necessary to plan and implement activities necessary to restore full, normal operations. Reconstitution activities are essential since the continuity situation cannot end until reconstitution is complete.

Essential Records

Essential records are those records (hard and soft copies, resources, information systems and applications, etc.) necessary to support performance of essential functions. These records include:

- Continuity plans
- Emergency operating procedures
- Critical reference files
- Emergency personnel lists (including backups)

- Emergency contracts
- Critical stakeholder and customer files
- **Reconstitution plans**

You should **NOT** limit essential records because of form or format.

Keep in mind that there is a difference between essential records (those needed to conduct continuity operations) and all records (which will be required for full reconstitution).

Human Resources

In a continuity activation, organizations will activate continuity personnel, referred to as the Emergency Relocation Group (ERG), and expect them to perform their assigned duties. The ERG is comprised of individuals who are assigned responsibility to relocate to an alternate site, as required, to perform organization essential functions or other tasks related to continuity operations.

In addition to supporting the human resources needs of continuity personnel, organizations are also responsible for supporting employees who are not designated as ERG personnel (referred to as non-ERG members), but who may also be affected by a continuity activation. Procedures and expectations for these employees should be addressed in continuity and emergency plans, such as the Occupant Emergency Plan, which includes evacuation and shelter-in-place planning.

Depending on the situation, many non-essential personnel may still be able to perform routine functions via telework, as long as their work does not interfere with or disrupt performance of the essential functions.

Although a lot of the staff (non-ERG personnel) may not be required to perform functions, accountability for all personnel is important. This is part of the essential function to protect and preserve resources (in this case, personnel resources).

Tests, Training, and Exercises

TT&E is necessary for all aspects of continuity, including reconstitution.

- ERG and support personnel must be trained.
- Emergency equipment must be tested.
- Organizations must exercise plans and procedures to:
    - Ensure and demonstrate preparedness.
    - Identify gaps and weaknesses.

- o Build organizational confidence and improve performance.
- o Be prepared.

Reconstitution

Reconstitution is one of the 10 elements of continuity. In addition, reconstitution:

- Is an essential function.
- Requires a plan and essential records.
- Involves essential personnel — the ERG team.
- Requires TT&E.

Keep in mind, continuity is focused on the most important and urgent functions, whereas reconstitution concerns EVERYTHING!

Additionally, only a select few people are directly involved in continuity operations (the ERG), whereas reconstitution planning involves everyone in the organization.

Reconstitution Defined

Reconstitution is defined as the process by which surviving and/or replacement agency personnel resume all normal agency operations from the original or replacement primary operating facility.

It allows an agency to recover from an event that disrupts normal operations and consolidates the necessary resources so that the agency can resume its operations as a fully functional entity. This may require coordination to procure a new operating facility and equipment. It may also require new or supplemental staffing.

Note: One approach to the "resume all normal agency operations" may be to look at the organization's situation just prior to the disruption. Depending on the severity of the disruption, however, some agencies may be faced with establishing a "new normal."

Scope of Reconstitution

Reconstitution can be as **simple** as offices being fully open following limited operations after a snowstorm and all employees expected to report to work for normal operations. Another example would be if an office had a fire and employees were informed they could return to work.

OR

Reconstitution can be as **complicated** as recovering from an attack such as the one on the World Trade Center, with challenges that include relocation of operations with survivors — first to a temporary location for full operations, and then to a new permanent location.

Reconstitution, as well as continuity, are ultimately about performing **FUNCTIONS**.

Reconstitution Planning

Reconstitution planning begins **now** as an element of a comprehensive continuity planning process.

The reconstitution manager should **not** be the continuity manager (if possible). Many organizations use a key staff member from facilities management, logistics, security, or similar functions to lead the reconstitution team.

Reconstitution activities should start very shortly after the activation of the continuity plan in order to begin consideration of the return to full and normal operations as quickly as possible.

Note: The reconstitution planning manager may or may not be the same person as the reconstitution implementation manager — this will be covered in more detail later in the course.

Summary

This concludes Lesson 1: Introduction and Course Overview.

This lesson:

- Provided the purpose of this course.
- Reviewed basic information on continuity.
- Introduced basic concepts of reconstitution.

In lesson 2, you will learn about reconstitution requirements.

Lesson 2 — Reconstitution Requirements

Overview

In this lesson, we will review the established Federal requirements for reconstitution found in National Continuity Policy Implementation Plan (NCPIP) and Federal Continuity Directive 1 (FCD 1). These requirements are mandatory for Federal executive branch departments and agencies. To the extent they apply, these requirements are recommended for State, territorial, tribal, and local (STTL) agencies.

Keep in mind, the Federal Government is not mandating compliance with these requirements for non-Federal entities. Some requirements, however, may be separately mandated through contracts or grant requirements. Additionally, some State and local governments have adopted the Federal requirements as their own.

Objectives

At the completion of this lesson, students will be able to do the following:

- Identify reconstitution plan requirements.
- Identify reconstitution implementation requirements.

National Continuity Policy

Let's begin by reviewing what the National Continuity Policy, also referred to as National Security Presidential Directive-51/Homeland Security Presidential Directive-20 (NSPD-51/HSPD-20), has to say about reconstitution.

NSPD-51/HSPD-20, Paragraph 11(f), states:

Continuity requirements for the Executive Office of the President (EOP) and executive branch departments and agencies shall include the following:

- Provision must be made for reconstitution capabilities that allow for recovery from a catastrophic emergency and resumption of normal operations.

Remember, reconstitution is one of the ten elements of continuity. This is important to note, as a continuity situation cannot end until all elements have been accomplished, with reconstitution being the last step!

Select this link for an accessible version of the NSPD-51/HSPD-20 PDF document.

NCPIP

The NCPIP also makes references to reconstitution, including:

- Plans and Procedures — Department and agency continuity plans must provide for the ability to recover or reconstitute from the effects of an emergency and return to a fully operational condition.
- Non-Federal organizations (STTL and Private Sector) are encouraged to develop a robust continuity program to ensure that essential functions are performed. These actions will permit timely reconstitution and recovery from catastrophic emergencies and resumption of normal operations.

Note: These items are required for Federal departments and agencies. They are encouraged for STTL governments. The Federal Government cannot dictate these kinds of requirements to local governments, however.

It may be worth noting that some Federal agencies are making the Federal continuity requirements mandatory for State and local governments as part of Federal grant money awards. This is similar to requirements to meet Federal standards if a State accepts Federal highway or education funding.

FCD 1 Requirements

Over the next several screens, we will focus on FCD 1 and the requirements it identifies for reconstitution.

FCD-1 (Section 9. j.) states:
Reconstitution is the process by which surviving and/or replacement organization personnel resume normal organization operations from the original or replacement primary operating facility. Reconstitution embodies the ability of an organization to recover from a continuity activation that disrupts normal operations so that the organization can resume its operations as a fully functional entity of the Federal Government. In some cases, extensive coordination may be necessary to backfill staff, procure a new operating facility, and re-establish communications, IT infrastructure, and essential records.

Note: You should review the requirements before taking on the process of evaluating or building a new reconstitution plan.

FCD 1 Requirements — Training and Exercise

Reconstitution plans require training and exercising. FCD 1 Annex K — Test, Training, and Exercise (TT&E) Program states:

An organization's training program must include:

- *15.b Annual training for ERG and DERG members on all reconstitution plans and procedures to resume normal organization operations at the original or primary operating facility or replacement primary operating facility.*

An organization's exercise program must include and document:

- *23. A biennial exercise for Emergency Relocation Group (ERG) members to demonstrate their familiarity with the reconstitution procedures to transition from a continuity environment to normal activities when appropriate.*

FCD 1 Requirements — Devolution

Keep in mind that there needs to be a backup reconstitution plan, i.e., a devolution plan, in case the disruption is so severe that the primary reconstitution team is not able to function effectively. FCD 1 Annex L — Devolution states:

A devolution plan will:

- *2. Organizations must address the following elements of a viable continuity capability in their devolution option: program plans and procedures, risk management, budgeting and acquisitions, essential functions, orders of succession and delegations of authority specific to the devolution site, continuity communications, essential records management, human resources, TT&E, and reconstitution.*

Note: The devolution reconstitution requirements will be covered in more detail later in this course.

FCD 1 Requirements — Reconstitution

The next several screens will cover reconstitution planning and implementation identified in FCD 1 Annex M — Reconstitution Operations.

When planning for reconstitution, FCD 1 Annex M — Reconstitution Operations states:

- *1. Organizations must develop a plan and provide the ability to recover from the effects of an emergency and for transitioning back to efficient normal operational status from continuity operations, once a threat or disruption has passed.*
- *2. Organizations must coordinate and pre-plan options for organization reconstitution regardless of the level of disruption that originally prompted the organization to implement its continuity plans.*
- *3. Organizations must designate a reconstitution manager and a devolution reconstitution manager (if the primary reconstitution manager is located at the primary operating facility) to oversee all phases of the reconstitution process.*

FCD 1 Requirements — Reconstitution (continued)

Reconstitution implementation is initiated by organization leadership. Following a significant disruption, it is not intended for individuals or components to start reconstitution on their own; it should be coordinated.

The focus should be on deliberate planning for reconstitution, or "smooth transition." This highlights a significant difference between reconstitution and continuity activation (which may take place with no warning and under crisis conditions).

It is very important to regularly communicate the status of your organization. For non-Federal entities, appropriate notifications should be made regarding continuity and reconstitution status. Some organizations have established formal notification requirements. If no such formal requirements exist, non-Federal entities may want to ask who is responsible for keeping track of continuity status and reconstitution progress.

Note: Various reconstitution options will be discussed in more detail in Lesson 3: Types of Reconstitution.

Select this link to review Annex M — Reconstitution Operations.

FCD 1 Requirements — Reconstitution (continued)

FCD 1 Annex N — Continuity Plan Operational Phases and Implementation states that organizations must do the following when implementing their continuity plans and procedures:

- *17. Identify all available organization leadership at the continuity facilities and conduct the orderly and pre-defined transition of leadership, for the position of Organization Head, as well as for key supporting positions, in accordance with orders of succession and delegations of authority, as applicable.*
- *19. Verify that all systems, communications, and other required capabilities are available and operational at the new or restored primary operating facility and that the organization is fully capable of performing all essential functions and operations at the new or restored primary operating facility.*

FCD 1 Requirements — Reconstitution (continued)

In addition, under FCD 1 Annex N — Continuity Plan Operational Phases and Implementation, when implementing their continuity plans and procedures organizations must:

- *21. Inform all personnel that the actual emergency, or the threat of an emergency, and the necessity for continuity operations no longer exists, and instruct personnel on how to resume normal operations.*
- *24. Determine which (if any) records were affected by the incident and ensure an effective transition or recovery of essential records and databases and other records that had not been designated as essential records.*

FCD 1 Requirements — Reconstitution (continued)

It is very important to regularly communicate the status of your organization. For non-Federal entities, appropriate notifications should be made regarding continuity and reconstitution status. Some organizations have established formal notification requirements. If no such formal requirements exist, non-Federal entities may want to ask who is responsible for keeping track of continuity status and reconstitution progress.

Keep in mind, leadership communicates instructions for resumption of normal operations to all staff, including supervising an orderly return to the normal operating facility, moving to another temporary facility, or to a new permanent facility. The process of reconstitution will generally start immediately after an event concludes. This information further emphasizes the deliberate and planned nature ("orderly return") of reconstitution.

Note: Contrary to the devolution process, which takes into account both **active** and **passive** triggers, there is no passive trigger for reconstitution.

Reconstitution Requirements — Planning Summary

The following is a summary of the reconstitution planning requirements:

- Federal executive branch organizations are required to have a reconstitution plan, and STTL and other organizations are strongly encouraged to have one.
- The ERG are required to exercise the reconstitution plan.
- A reconstitution exercise is to be held biennially.
- The reconstitution plan must include procedures for conducting a smooth transition to full operations and capabilities.

Reconstitution Requirements — Implementation Summary

The following is a summary of the reconstitution implementation requirements:

- Instruct personnel on how to return to normal operations.
- Verify that all systems and capabilities are operational.
- Supervise an orderly return to work.
- Notification(s) that reconstitution has occurred must be made.
- Ensure an effective transition or recovery of essential records (and, in fact, all records).
- Conduct an after action review, identify areas for improvement, establish a CAP, and develop a remedial action plan.

Keep in mind, most of the Federal reconstitution requirements are really just good business practices and would apply to any organization.

Reconstitution Requirements Summary

The Federal reconstitution requirements establish broad guidance, but specific details regarding reconstitution are left up to individual organizations and may vary considerably depending on the organization, its missions, its people, its location(s), and the particular disruptions that might occur.

Remember to consider other "requirements" that might be worth adding to the list for your organization!

Continuity Readiness Cell

FEMA's National Continuity Programs have established a Continuity Readiness Cell (CRC) structure to:

- Monitor and report continuity status of Federal executive branch Headquarters departments and agencies.
- Assess potential impact(s) to continuity of operations.
- Facilitate information sharing among operational nodes of the Federal Government.
- Provide continuity input to the DHS Common Operating Picture.
- Monitor the operation of continuity communications systems.
- Assist with reconstitution of the Federal executive branch.

Consider the situation in which multiple agencies have activated their continuity plans, which may complicate partnership communications. The CRC can help resolve communications difficulties.

Note: Regional Federal executive branch offices should coordinate with their headquarters to determine if reports to the CRC are necessary.

Continuity Status Report

The Continuity Status Report (CSR) provides up-to-date status information that is needed for the CRC. Specifically, the CSR:

- Provides interagency depiction of Federal continuity capabilities and readiness. (This information is updated before, during, and after an event.)
- Reports:
    - Operational status (including Continuity of Government [COGCON] level).
    - Ability to perform essential functions.
    - Operational location.
    - Continuity of operations, devolution, and/or reconstitution status.

Summary

This concludes the lesson on reconstitution requirements. You should now be able to do the following:

- Describe the role of reconstitution in overall continuity.
- Identify reconstitution plan requirements.

- Identify reconstitution implementation requirements.

In lesson 3, you will learn about different types of reconstitution planning.

Lesson 3 — Types of Reconstitution

Overview

This lesson will cover situations in which reconstitution is necessary, as well as different types of reconstitution.

We will also identify planning considerations for each type of reconstitution.

Lesson Objectives

At the completion of this lesson, students will be able to do the following:

- Describe when reconstitution may be required.
- Identify different types of reconstitution.
- Identify the four different phases of reconstitution.

When is Reconstitution Necessary?

Examples of events that could cause disruptions requiring reconstitution include:

- Facilities or buildings damaged due to a terrorist attack, an earthquake, a hurricane, etc.
- Access restricted due to public transportation disruption, flooding, wildfire, etc.
- Infrastructure disruptions caused by a power outage, cyber attack, etc.
- Impact on personnel due to a pandemic, biological attack, etc.

Keep in mind, some disruptions will primarily affect the facilities, some disruptions will primarily affect people, some disruptions will affect supporting infrastructure, and some disruptions will affect a combination of each. The reconstitution plan will need to address all of these, and the approach may vary considerably, depending on the events that lead up to it.

Disruptions

When thinking about disruptions, you should focus first on disruptions to the performance of operations or functions (as opposed to community disruptions). A transit strike might create some delays and annoyance **or** it might shut down a city and prevent an organization from doing its job. From a continuity perspective, it's important to focus on disruptions that impact operations.

Types of disruptions may include:

- Facility: Electrical, communications, water, climate control, fire, structural, physical security, etc.
- Data: Servers, virus, backup/storage, software applications, etc.
- Nature: Natural disasters, meteorological events, etc.
- Human (external or internal): Terrorism/sabotage, virus attack, operations mistakes, active shooter, etc.
- Suppliers: Supply chain could be interrupted.

Types of Reconstitution Planning

Planning for reconstitution requires consideration of several possible reconstitution alternatives:

Primary Facilities Reconstitution

This is the process of returning to full, normal operations at the original (possibly repaired) facility. This situation would generally occur when primary operating facilities are not significantly impacted by disruptions. These disruptions may include a snowstorm, labor strike, mass transit disruption, pandemic, localized fire, etc.

Note: This may also be the case (consider the Pentagon) where a facility is an icon and may be repaired even if there is extensive damage — but the repairs may take a very long time. So, reconstitution may have to occur using long-term temporary facilities.

Temporary Facilities Reconstitution

This is the process of returning to full operations at temporary (possibly distributed) facilities, with the expectation of moving to new or repaired facilities when they can be made available. This situation might occur when there is significant damage to the primary facilities, or when repairs are either not feasible or economical, or will take an extended period of time (i.e., more than 6 months). Nevertheless, full operations (performing all functions) may be possible in a temporary rented space. Examples include a significant building fire, an earthquake, or a terrorist attack that significantly damages or contaminates the facilities.

Note: The anthrax attacks on Senate offices and other facilities in the fall of 2001 resulted in a number of buildings being closed for an extended period of time. Agency work was suspended and then reconstituted in temporary facilities until the original facilities could be cleaned and made safe.

New Facilities Reconstitution

This is the process of restoring full operations at permanent replacement facilities. This may be preceded by operations at temporary or interim facilities. If replacement facilities are readily available (for example, a small organization that normally operates from a rented office space), it may be possible to move directly from continuity operations to new permanent facilities.

Note: "New" facilities could also be constructed on the old site.

Executive branch departments and agencies are required to develop plans to deal with all three types of reconstitution.

Phases of Reconstitution

Reconstitution can be divided into four phases:

1. Pre-event preparedness planning (normal operations)
2. Post-event planning (continuity operations)
3. Reconstitution implementation (execution and transition)
4. Reconstitution completion (resumption of full, normal operations and post-reconstitution activities)

The change from normal to continuity operations is generally sudden and the organization is in crisis mode.

Remember, the "event" is the disruption that causes activation of the continuity plan. This is the point at which the nature of operations changes.

In contrast to activating continuity, reconstitution is generally gradual and deliberate. Although the initial portions of reconstitution (assessment and planning) may begin during the early stages of continuity operations, implementing reconstitution will typically take place on a "good day."

Pre-Event Reconstitution Planning

Pre-event reconstitution planning takes place now (during "good" conditions). This planning includes:

- Developing an all hazards reconstitution plan including:

- o Identifying what might need to be done (i.e., checklists).
    - o Identifying who will need to do it (i.e., rosters).
    - o Generating or gathering records necessary to implement the plan.
- Obtaining approval of the plan.
- Conducting training and exercises for the plan.
- Identifying lessons learned from the exercises and refining the plan.

Pre-event planning is for all hazards. We do not know what will happen and what impact it may have, thus we have to prepare for everything.

Post-Event Reconstitution Planning

Post-event reconstitution planning takes place right after both the disruption and activation of continuity have occurred. It is a continuity activity, where planning will be focused on the specific event that happened. It is no longer an "all hazards" effort. During this planning:

- Begin with an assessment of the situation:
    - o How much damage has been done?
    - o Do you return to the original facilities or stay at the new?
    - o Is there a need to replace staff?
- Take the plan and begin to refine it (being very specific):
    - o How long will repairs take?
    - o Are temporary facilities needed?
    - o Will partial devolution be implemented for some functions?

Note: Post-event planning may be incremental (i.e., plan a procedure, then implement that procedure; plan the next procedure, then implement that one; etc.). Post-event planning and implementation, however, may be cyclic.

Reconstitution is an Essential Function

As an element of continuity, reconstitution must be considered as an essential function that ensures the continued support for performance of MEFs and the restoration of full normal operations.

Reconstitution activities generally begin upon arrival at the continuity site. It is a full-time effort!

Some ERG members are identified to support the performance of organizational MEFs during a continuity event. Remember, the reconstitution team personnel are ERG members dedicated to the resumption of full and normal activities. However, it is important that ERG personnel who are performing the essential functions are not distracted with other duties. Thus, a separate reconstitution team should be identified.

Note: Many small organizations as well as state and local organizations may not have the personnel to create separate teams. In this case, organizations should at least have separate managers so the reconstitution manager can focus on that job, even if some of the team members have multiple responsibilities.

Reconstitution Implementation

The following is a list of Federal requirements for implementing reconstitution:

- A priority-based approach must be used.
- MEFs must not be disrupted.
- All personnel need to be informed of the plan and expectations.
- Instructions for resumption of normal operations (including supervising an orderly return to the original facility, or moving to temporary or new permanent facilities) must be provided.
- Update/transition records during the continuity event as part of the full recovery of all records.
- Partners, customers, and stakeholders must be kept informed.
- Regular status updates must be provided.
- Agency's status must be reported to the CRC.

Note: Non-Federal entities may have somewhat different requirements.

Reconstitution Implementation Process

Reconstitution implementation is a planned and deliberate process. Implementation actions associated with reconstitution include:

1. Provide information and instructions to agency personnel on how to resume normal operations.
2. Supervise an orderly return to original work location(s), temporary facilities, or new permanent facilities.
3. Verify that all systems, communications, and required capabilities are available and operational.
4. Provide Reconstitution Status Report(s) on reconstitution status.
5. Update/transition records created during the continuity event as a part of the full recovery of all records.
6. Restore continuity facilities to full readiness capability.

7. Complete after action report/improvement plan (AAR/IP) for CAP implementation.

Reconstitution Completion

Once reconstitution is complete, there are several post-reconstitution activities that need to be accomplished. This includes:

1. Validating that full normal operations are being successfully conducted, full capabilities have been restored, and normal steady state operations can continue.
2. Completing a Reconstitution Status Report indicating reconstitution is complete (for reconstitution manager).
3. Developing an AAR/IP and tracking results in the CAP.
4. Reviewing continuity and reconstitution plans, and updating them to reflect lessons learned.

Defining Successful Reconstitution

Each organization will have to establish its own criteria for when they will consider that reconstitution has been accomplished, or reached an end state. Possible criteria include:

- Restoration of full organization functionality — performing all agency functions needs to be done somewhere, anywhere
- Performing all organizational functions under normal conditions for an extended period of time
- Performing all functions in permanent (new or repaired) facilities

Defining Successful Reconstitution (continued)

Accomplishing reconstitution is not as simple as it may seem. You must understand that there are differences among each of the possible end states. For example, if an organization is able to restore full functionality (of all functions) using extensive telework and with staff spread among various facilities in various locations, including some shift work, does this complete the reconstitution process? Or does the organization believe that all of its personnel should be working regular hours in the same building or complex in order for reconstitution to be considered complete?

There is no one clear answer to this question and it may depend on the size and type of organization. This is a question each organization will have to address based on its mission and situation.

Summary

This concludes the lesson on types of reconstitution. You should now be able to do the following:

- Describe when reconstitution may be required.
- Identify different types of reconstitution.
- Identify the four different phases of reconstitution.

In lesson 4, you will learn about reconstitution teams.

Lesson 4 — Reconstitution Teams

Overview

In this lesson we will identify which positions are required for the reconstitution planning team, as well as which positions are required for the reconstitution implementation team. We will also distinguish the differences between the two.

Keep in mind that when staffing your teams, you should be sensitive to the distinction between the open positions and the specific personnel who must fill them. For example, positions that need to be filled may include an HR manager or a lawyer. The personnel must have the experience and background to take on these positions.

Another example could be when an organization determines that a contracts lawyer should be included on the reconstitution team. The next question for the organization may be which contracts lawyer (from among the several on staff) can best serve as an ERG member (someone who can deploy, leave family, work under "continuity" conditions, etc.).

Lesson Objectives

At the completion of this lesson, students will be able to do the following:

- Identify the responsibilities of the reconstitution manager.
- Identify who should be on the reconstitution planning team.
- Identify the goals of the reconstitution planning team.

- Identify who should be on the reconstitution implementation team.
- Identify the work that must be conducted by the reconstitution implementation team.

Reconstitution Teams

The reconstitution team is part of the ERG and is responsible for performing the essential function of returning the organization to normal operations at a new or restored facility.

Leadership must designate a senior member of the organization to be responsible for reconstitution — this is the reconstitution manager.

The reconstitution planning team (pre-event) needs to be pre-identified to gather information and develop processes to address a wide variety of situations as we cannot predict what event might happen to the organization.

The implementation (or operational) team needs to be pre-identified to more precisely determine problems and solutions affecting the organization after the initial event.

You will learn more about these teams as you proceed through this lesson.

Note: It should be recognized that many smaller organizations and State and local governments may not have sufficient personnel or resources to support multiple teams. These organizations should consider cross-training personnel or devolving functions to an area that is not operating under emergency conditions.

The Reconstitution Manager

Every organization should identify a reconstitution manager. One thing a reconstitution manager must understand is that planning for reconstitution and implementing reconstitution are two very different things. However, the reconstitution manager will oversee both the pre-event and post-event reconstitution elements and direct the planning and implementation reconstitution teams.

The reconstitution manager should:

- Be able to focus solely on the issues related to reconstitution during a continuity event — no other job!
- Have a close working relationship with the continuity manager.
- Be senior enough to work directly with senior leadership.
- Be familiar with the reconstitution plan.
- Be able to lead a reconstitution team.

- Be detail oriented.

Note: Although departments and agencies should identify a reconstitution manager to plan and manage day-to-day reconstitution activities, ultimate responsibility goes to senior leadership. They should empower the reconstitution manager so he or she can get the job done!

Reconstitution Planning Team

The success of your reconstitution planning and implementation may depend on the membership of the reconstitution planning team. When developing your team, consider adding members from areas including, but not limited to:

- Senior leadership
- Facilities/logistics
- Information technology (IT)
- Communications
- Human resources
- Operations
- Security

Reconstitution Planning (Pre-event)

- The organization will accept.
- Leadership will approve.
- Can be trained and exercised throughout the organization.
- Will provide a reasonable and useful starting point for the post-event planning team to get the job done if a disruption occurs.

Reconstitution Planning (Pre-event) (continued)

Remember, continuity is focused on a small but very critical set of functions that cannot be deferred, whereas reconstitution must consider **ALL** organizational functions.

Reconstitution planning will require effort by every office and group in the organization. If disaster strikes and people do not survive, records are lost, and equipment and facilities become unavailable, there needs to be sufficient resources and guidance available to reconstitute **EVERY** government function. Thus, every office that performs a government function will need to document what they do, how they do it, and in some cases, why it is important (though perhaps not urgent).

This may be a bigger task for unusual functions that very few people perform (e.g., particular technical functions unique to the organization), as opposed to more common functions (e.g., contracting, security, motor pool, human resources management) that most organizations perform.

Given the difficulty with larger working groups, there may be a benefit to having a core group that focuses on most of the planning effort, and bringing in various subject matter experts as they are needed. But having a large group engaged in the process will also help market and socialize the plan. Organizational buy-in will be important.

Reconstitution Implementation Team

The implementation or operational team first order of business is to refine the pre-event reconstitution plan to fit the circumstances. This team should be comprised of planners and implementers. Therefore, it may be necessary to defer on deciding the complete make-up of the reconstitution implementation team until the situation can be fully assessed (post-event). Some membership on the implementation team will be determined by the tasks that will be required. In some cases, the team may be heavy on the facilities management side. In other situations, it may be more focused on human resources. In any case, all aspects will need to be addressed and potential team members will need to be put on notice.

Some of the work the reconstitution implementation team will need to perform will include:

- Assessing the actual situation
- Refining the reconstitution plan
- Getting approval of the plan
- Communicating the plan
- Implementing the plan

Personnel who will be serving on the reconstitution implementation team need to know that they will be members of the ERG and will need to make plans accordingly.

Reconstitution Implementation Team (continued)

Review the following event:

Over the weekend, a fire destroyed the east wing of your agency. The fire marshal states that the west wing of the building is able to function. The continuity plan has been activated and ERG members have relocated to the continuity site to continue essential functions. The reconstitution manager has met with his team. What reconstitution actions will the team take to determine and continue the agency's operations during the restoration process?

Based on this event the following list is just some of the examples of the information that the reconstitution implementation team will need:

- What is the degree of damage? Can equipment/supplies be salvaged? When can the east wing be recoccupied? (Facilities)
- Can employees access the building? (Security)
- What systems are available to employees in the west wing? (IT, Facilities, Records)
- What personnel are affected by the damage? Can those affected telework? Do they have equipment? (HR, IT)
- When will the building be restored? (Facilities)
- How will employees be kept informed of the agency's status? (HR)
- What other items need to be considered during the reconstitution process?

Note: Each organization will have to determine what their reconstitution steps will include in order to meet FCD 1 requirements. The level of disruption could be from a small fire to an active shooter to an area-wide natural disaster.

Reconstitution Implementation Team (continued)

The reconstitution implementation team will conduct its work at either the alternate site or at another facility.

Not all agencies send their reconstitution team ERG members to the same location as those performing the MEFs. Planners need to decide what approach makes sense for their organization and what their leadership will want.

During an event, resources the reconstitution implementation team may/will require includes supplies they need to conduct the essential functions, systems and records they need to access, etc.

In addition, are they running 24/7 operations? If so, does the ERG stay on site in housing, or is lodging available close to the alternate facility? Is there a dining facility on site or do they need to go off site to eat? Is there security on site?

Reconstitution Operational Team

The reconstitution manager identifies, coordinates, and trains personnel who will support reconstitution operations. Reconstitution planning members (or team) support development of the reconstitution plan and the processes and procedures necessary to resume operations at the primary, temporary, or new/rebuilt facility.

Once a continuity event is called and the operational phase of continuity is implemented, reconstitution begins. The operational reconstitution team is the ERG who now carry out the reconstitution plan. It is possible an agency might have agreements with external partners (structural engineers, HVAC, etc.) to assist with the operational phase (Those entities actually carrying out the econstitution efforts.).

The reconstitution team may have completed all of the planning, writing procedures, etc., but the operational team implements the plan.

Reconstitution from Devolution

Special consideration needs to be given to the possibility that some or all of an organization's functions may have to be reconstituted by the devolution team.

This presents some unique challenges that you will need to consider:

- Does your devolution team have a reconstitution element?
- Does the devolution reconstitution team need to be co-located with the devolution team that will be performing essential functions?
- What special training does the devolution reconstitution team require?

Devolution Reconstitution Team

The devolution reconstitution team are the members of the devolution emergency relocation group (DERG) who will assume the duties of the reconstitution ERG members at the headquarters facility.

Summary

This concludes the lesson on reconstitution teams. You should now be able to do the following:

- Identify the responsibilities of the reconstitution manager.
- Identify who should be on the reconstitution planning team.
- Identify the goals of the reconstitution planning team.

- Identify who should be on the reconstitution implementation team.
- Identify the work that must be conducted by the reconstitution implementation team.

In lesson 5, you will learn about the elements of reconstitution.

Lesson 5 — Elements of Reconstitution

Overview

In this lesson we we will identify and consider the full range of reconstitution elements.

We will also determine the requirements needed to transition or recover both essential functions and non-essential functions.

Lesson Objectives

At the completion of this lesson, students will be able to do the following:

- Identify the major elements of a comprehensive reconstitution plan.
- Describe the requirements for each element of the plan.

The Major Elements of Reconstitution

Previously, we have reviewed the requirements for reconstitution, discussed various types of reconstitution, and identified who should be involved in reconstitution planning. At this time, we will begin to outline the major elements that will have to be considered as we build a reconstitution plan.

Some examples of reconstitution elements include:

- People:
    - Leadership
    - Staff
    - Periodic communications
- Communications:
    - Employees
    - ERG
    - Partners
    - Stakeholders
- Facilities
- Records
- Functions:
    - Essential functions (MEFs and ESAs)
    - Other functions

Note: State and local organizations may have different requirements than Federal agencies. In addition, small Federal agencies may have different requirements than large Federal agencies.

Reconstitution Elements

Some examples of broader categories of elements you will need to address in your reconstitution plan(s) include:

- People — What personnel will need to be included?
- Security — Are measures in place to provide for personnel, computer, and network security?
- Communications — Are they interoperable and redundant? Is the workforce knowledgeable on the agency's alert and notification procedures?
- TTE — Do ERG members receive training annually? Does the ERG test the COOP plan annually; do they include a relocation exercises?
- Human Resources — Are personnel aware of pay, leave, benefits, overtime policies, etc.
- Essential Records — Are essential records backed up daily to a COOP server? Is there a records plan for coop records? Is there a contract with a records recovery company?

Reconstitution Element: Plans (Pre-Event)

Since we do not know what the disruption may be, when it may happen, or what and who it may impact, the (pre-event) reconstitution plan, which is developed now, will need to address all of the elements that may need to be considered for your organization. Remember, the plan must include policies, procedures, checklists, and TT&E requirements.

While there will be many aspects of reconstitution plans that are common to all organizations, every plan will be unique to meet the needs of a specific organization. This will be a general plan from which an operational plan, completed by the reconstitution implementation team (post-event), will be constructed after the disruption occurs. It is very unlikely that the pre-event plan will suffice as an operational plan after a significant disruption. Understanding this will help shape the pre-event plan.

It is also important that the operational reconstitution team (the group that will report as part of the ERG to plan and implement reconstitution) understands the purpose of the pre-event plan and how that will guide them. That being said, the operational reconstitution team must be part of the planning effort.

Reconstitution Element: Status

After a disruption occurs, **as soon as possible**, the operational reconstitution team will need an accurate assessment of the situation in order to determine how and when reconstitution can occur, as well as when to begin creating an operational plan. An assessment should ask the following questions:

- Is the crisis over?
- Are all personnel accounted for and safe?
  - Will replacement personnel be needed?
- Are the facilities damaged?
  - Will repairs be needed?
  - How complicated will repairs be?
- Will temporary or new facilities be needed?
- Are there unique assessment considerations that need to be addressed?
- What other status issues should be included?

Identify who (which organization) is responsible for answering each of these questions!

Reconstitution Element: Plans (Post-Event)

The (post-event) reconstitution plan will have to be written (built) after the disruption has occurred and will be based on the actual situation as it exists. For example, the plan should describe the:

- Damage that was done and what repairs are needed
- Impact on people
- Functions that were disrupted

There will be many more questions to answer and the post-event planning team will need to start with the pre-event reconstitution plan and build an operational plan to be implemented.

Reconstitution Element: Plans (Post-Event) (continued)

Post-event reconstitution planning will require:

- Leadership — reconstitution manager
- Team members
- Facilities — working space

- Information — assessment and status
- Senior Leadership support and guidance

Post-event planning may be conducted at the organization's continuity or alternate facility, or it could be conducted at another location. In any case, the plan should identify the core personnel who will be on the team and where they are expected to report. Others will have to be added as needed (supplemental or associate reconstitution team members), based on the actual situation and the associated requirements.

Note: An important distinction between activating a continuity plan in the first place and implementing reconstitution is urgency. Although there will be pressure to reconstitute quickly, there will be far less urgency and uncertainty. It should be a deliberate and methodical process based on solid information.

Reconstitution Element: Milestones

Based on the pre-event reconstitution plan, the disruption that occurred and the assessment of its impact on the organization, and the guidance from organizational leadership the post-event reconstitution planning team will need to establish or refine a series of operational reconstitution milestones.

The operational reconstitution milestones will probably be refined as the process proceeds and additional information becomes available. Establishing a schedule with target dates, however, will be important to ensuring all of the pieces are in place to reconstitute all of the organizational functions in a logical order.

Reconstitution Element: Milestones (continued)

The reconstitution planning team should develop milestones that, at a minimum, include:

- Assessment of the situation and the primary facility
- Status of personnel
- Coordination for facilities (temporary or new), if needed
- Communications, reporting, and messaging
- Projected end of the crisis or emergency
- Equipment and logistics issues
- Update and recovery of records
- Transfer of essential functions and key supporting activities
- Implementation of full reconstitution of functions

Note: Additional milestones may include demobilization of the continuity facility and its operation, including bringing the functions and people from the alternate site back to the repaired or new facility, and recovering equipment that had been used at the alternate facility. Equally important is restocking and preparing the alternate facility in case another continuity event occurs.

Reconstitution Element: People

People will be one of the most critical elements of reconstitution and potentially the most complicated (depending on the event). For most organizations, it will be important to include experienced (senior) HR representation on the reconstitution team for both planning and implementation. Also, functions cannot be reconstituted if the right people are not available, trained, and qualified to do the work.

People will need to communicate with each of the functional areas to verify that human capital resources are available:

- Are new hires needed?
- Is training or certification needed?

The reconstitution team should seek assistance from their human resources office and possibly from OPM (or the equivalent for non-Federal organizations).

Reconstitution Element: People (continued)

Until all of the staff returns to work, there may be issues regarding pay, benefits, vacation, etc., that may need to be addressed. In some cases, employees may choose to retire or otherwise not return to work.

There also may be concerns about fairness — some employees may be required to work overtime (ERG and other supporting personnel), while some may be paid, but not required to work or allowed to telework.

Finally, clear policy guidance and frequent (or at least periodic) communications with all of the staff will be critical to minimizing employee concerns during a very high stress period. The potential for concern about these issues should not be underestimated. To minimize these issues, make sure you identify:

- Who should be responsible for ensuring effective communications.
- What information should be communicated.
- What modes of communications will be used.

Reconstitution Element: Facilities

A key step in reconstitution planning is to determine the condition of the facility after the event. Performing a detailed damage assessment may be beyond the expertise of the reconstitution team, however. It may require information from a structural engineer or other similar experts. The General Services Administration (GSA) is the lead Federal agency for reconstitution assistance with facilities. GSA may be able to provide acquisition assistance to include facilities and equipment for Federal agencies, and in some cases, for State and local organizations as well. Federal assistance for State and locals may be available through GSA, depending on Stafford Act declaration.

Note: There may be a requirement to work with local government officials before facilities can be repaired, modified, and/or occupied. Reconstitution planners should understand these issues before an event occurs and know who they will need to talk to.

Facilities: Repairs

If it is determined from the damage assessment that the facilities can be repaired, this process can be hastened if the reconstitution plan includes information that will support the process.

To hasten repairs, the reconstitution plan should identify key facilities personnel, where important documents can be found, and what resources may be required, including:

- Blueprints of existing facilities
- Requirements for wiring, IT, secure spaces
- Repair plans
- Contracts to initiate repairs
- Coordination with GSA/landlords

Keep in mind, repairs will need to be monitored and progress will need to be reported regularly to leadership and employees. In addition, the facilities experts in most organizations (or GSA) should be in charge of this effort.

Reconstitution Element: Temporary Space

Understanding options and exploring in advance what each organization can and cannot do on their own may save considerable time and frustration in a post-event environment. Consider the situation in which a number of agencies are disrupted at the same time. Those that are able to move quickly (because they did their homework in advance) may get the best or only temporary spaces/facilities available, leaving others with complex problems to solve.

The temporary space may be needed to reconstitute some or all functions if repairs will not be quick. Options for temporary space include:

- Facilities the organization already controls or manages.
- Arrangements for temporary space you can make on your own.
- Arrangements for temporary space through GSA.

GSA Support to Acquire Space

GSA is responsible for Federal space management and has developed, as a planning tool, forms to support space management planning for reconstitution. The forms are available on the GSA Web site.

GSA has knowledge of the market and available space. It operates with proven methods of space design that result in efficient work environments.

Early joint planning shortens and simplifies the delivery process at the most reasonable cost to the Government. GSA understands that needs may change during the delivery process and can assist in addressing requirement changes.

Note: If a temporary or new space is to be used, an appropriate risk assessment may need to be performed to ensure employee and operational safety. The reconstitution team should address how to make arrangements for this.

Temporary Space — Alternatives

Other strategies may need to be developed until adequate facilities are available. This may include shift work, desk sharing, and/or telework.

Shuttle services between other existing organizational facilities may need to be provided, as transportation may be limited following a severe disruption. At this point, you may need to consider the use of supplemental staffing that could be available in regional or field offices.

In general, this is an area where being creative can pay large dividends — but the staff will have to be flexible.

Understanding where your organization's staff live may play a role in determining what are acceptable facilities and locations for those facilities, and what will not work for your staff. An important question will be what commuting time and distance will be required for current employees.

Procedures to Request Space

GSA will need to know:

- The geographic area that is acceptable.
- Locations you are willing to place your office.
- Estimated total square footage.
- How long you need the space.
- Who will occupy the space.
- Special building features that might limit suitable properties.

The forms that GSA uses will provide a means to record this required information.

Note: Organizations may need to consider staff commuting requirements (where the staff lives, mass transit, highways and accessibility, parking, safety) as a factor in acceptable locations for temporary or new facilities.

New Facilities

If the original facilities will not be repaired, the new facilities will need to accommodate the following:

- Size and footprint to support returning personnel
- Location considerations:
    - Near existing staff, proximate to partners
    - Convenient to mass transit
    - Security considerations, risk assessment
- Improvements and changes from the original facilities

Considering some of these issues in advance will speed up the process of making arrangements for both temporary and new permanent facilities.

Note: GSA will be a critical partner in arranging new facilities for Federal agencies.

Reconstitution Element: Functions

Continuity is all about continuing to perform essential functions! Reconstitution, however, is about restoring functions!

When it comes to prioritizing the missions keep in mind:

- MEFs and ESAs must be continued.
- Reconstitution of additional functions will be priority based.
- The priorities must be identified.
- What will be required to support each mission must be identified.
- What will determine prioritization must be identified.

The order in which functions are recovered may depend on a number of factors, such as:

- Leadership priorities
- Interdependencies
- Partners
- Available space and staff

Resumption of Government Functions

Resuming Government functions requires the continuous support of MEFs and ESAs that are being accomplished by the ERG.

Keeping this in mind, the reconstitution effort will need to focus on resuming other functions that were interrupted and differed (i.e., those Government functions that are not MEFs and ESAs — everything else!).

Remember, during the reconstitution effort, consider interdependencies and support relationships that must be in place, including key partners, non-Federal agencies, and the private sector.

Transfer of Mission Essential Functions

Although the MEFs are among the most important functions the ERG performs, it may be best to reconstitute other functions at the original or new facility before moving the MEFs. In addition, supporting activities should be up and running before moving MEF operations to the original or new facility.

If the MEFs are being accomplished, there should be no rush to "fix" something that is working.

You should NOT move the performance of the most critical functions (MEFs) back to the repaired facility if the repaired facility cannot actually sustain support for those functions!

Reconstitution Element: Communications

The reconstitution of communications involves the following:

- Ensuring phones, support, etc., are all available:
    - Special equipment may include a communicator, conference lines, etc.
- Securing information technology (IT):
    - Equipment (servers, networks, VPNs, printers, etc.) up and running
    - Contractors (support services) available
    - Security, such as firewalls, set up
- A detailed inventory should already exist — who is the POC?

This may involve more than one reconstitution team member or point of contact. Every point of contact should have at least one back up.

Reconstitution Element: Communications (continued)

Interoperable and available communications capabilities in sufficient quantity and mode/media must be done in conjunction with the organization's operational requirements.

If possible, provide any unique communication capabilities that can support the organization's senior leadership under routine situations at the primary facility, remotely, while they are in transit, etc.

Note: Communications and IT equipment lists are likely dispersed throughout several (or many) organizations within each agency. It may take some effort to identify where all of the various lists are and who is responsible for them. Some of this information may be classified. An important part of the reconstitution planning process will be identifying where all of this information is located and who is responsible for ensuring it remains current.

Reconstitution Element: Messaging

A plan for reporting the operating status of the Agency must be developed. This plan includes coordinating messaging with staff, partners, customers, and stakeholders. The communication can be done through any medium, such as emails, newsletters, town hall meetings, senior leadership outreach, etc. The information that is presented can include:

- Stating if the threat no longer exists
- Letting personnel know that the location is safe to enter
- Any changes in support (cafeteria, gym, childcare, parking)

Reconstitution Element: Messaging (continued)

There will be a lot of reporting and messaging required and sought out. It will be important to identify ahead of time:

- Who will do this messaging?
- Who will approve the message?
- How frequently should it be done?
- What information should be given?
- Who are the recipients?

It will also be important to be ready to adjust as the situation dictates and evolves. The reconstitution plan should address this, and it should be consistent with the organization leadership's perspective on what is necessary and appropriate.

Reconstitution Element: Messaging (continued)

Those receiving communications should include:

- Employees:
  - Currently working (ERG and others)
  - Currently not working
- Contractors
- Customers
- Partners
- Stakeholders
- Local government
- Neighbors
- Media
- Social media

Reporting and Messaging

Reconstitution plans should be coordinated with local government, neighboring facilities, and the local community since activities may have an impact on traffic, local businesses, local police, and fire departments.

Keep in mind, if adjacent facilities were impacted, their plans may impact your organization — information sharing and coordination may help avoid difficulties and confusion.

Note: The public affairs and government (Congressional) affairs office(s) will want to play a role in developing and delivering external messages.

Reconstitution Element: Security

Security personnel should be part of many aspects of reconstitution and should probably be part of the planning team(s).

Security refers to:

- Physical security (guards, access, badging) issues
- Communications security issues

Security is required for:

- Personnel
- Facilities
- Personally identifiable information (PII)

Security includes:

- Classification
- PII
- Sensitive unclassified

Reconstitution Element: Safety

Occupational safety and health (OSH) personnel will want to participate in planning and implementation decisions regarding reconstituting safety standards.

OSH standards provide safety for personnel and facilities. These standards:

- Need to be in place and operational before people return.
- Need to address safety issues with personnel.
- Identify healthcare capabilities.
- Involve operations at the new facility and transportation to and from work.
- Provide a plan for testing safety systems.
- Identify any modifications needed for occupant emergency plans (OEP).

Reconstitution Element: Records

Records and documents, and access to them, are essential to all aspects of Government work. Records management will include:

- Preserving all of the organization's records until reconstitution is complete.
- Ensuring access to essential records during the continuity situation.
- Capturing records created during the disruption and during continuity operations:
  - These records are incorporated into the organization's records management system.

While the continuity team will be primarily concerned with "essential" records, the reconstitution team will need to be concerned about ALL records!

Reconstitution Element: Records (continued)

Access to systems and records needs to be in place before and as reconstitution occurs. Historical files (microfiche, hard copy, old computer tapes, etc.) must be preserved and accessible. Although there will likely be a records management organization, there will need to be a partnership among IT, security, HR, contracts, legal, and other organizations to make this work. It may be useful to establish a planning subgroup of the reconstitution team to address records management issues.

Keep in mind:

- Records created during the disruption need to be captured.
- Records inventories must be prepared.
- Records will need to be archived.

Note: You must find an appropriate means to record new work that is, or will be, conducted.

Reconstitution Element: Records (continued)

Some data may have been lost, and the identification of lost data will be critical to resuming functions at the primary facility. Recovery can be a very difficult task. The reconstitution strategy should include pre-identification of records recovery experts and vendors.

Even if no data has been lost, some data will have been created or updated during continuity operations. Measures should be taken to ensure that the data transferred is up to date.

The reconstitution team should seek preservation, scientific/technical, and records and archival advice and information for stabilization, security, logistics, and contracting for recovery services for damaged records from the **National Archives and Records Administration (NARA)** or the office of the local State archivist.

Reconstitution Element: Records (continued)

Infrastructure may be a concern to some organizations, particularly large organizations that may operate on a campus environment. This may include:

- Transportation of equipment and supplies
- Transportation of personnel
- Power systems
- Mail services
- Motor pool
- Warehouses and storage
- Printing and publishing

As the infrastructure that supports your organization is restored, testing will become an important element. It will be important to ensure that the infrastructure is fully operational and performing as required before transitioning critical functions and personnel. A comprehensive testing protocol should be in place and included in the reconstitution milestones.

Reporting Reconstitution Status

As various organizational elements begin to reconstitute their functions, the reconstitution team will want to track progress using a standardized approach so that the information can be consolidated and the status can be reported to leadership and the rest of the organization. This should include what is on target and what obstacles are impeding progress. Restoration of some activities may need to be sequential; the milestones checklist should identify this.

For Federal agencies, gathering this information will support status updates to the CRC. Similarly, at the State and local level, this will support whatever local reporting requirements need to be satisfied.

Declaring Reconstitution Success

Reconstitution is complete when:

- All organizational functions have been restored and are being performed, or
- All organizational functions have been restored and are being performed at temporary facilities that can support continued operations, or
- All organizational functions have been restored and are being performed at permanent facilities.

Reconstitution Element: Continuity

An interesting reconstitution challenge may be demobilization of the ERG and the alternate facility where the ERG was working.

Once the essential functions are transitioned out of the alternate facility, the alternate facility will need to be "reset" and prepared for the next continuity event. This requires:

- Removing unneeded or inoperable equipment.
- Restocking supplies and fuel.

Typically, this is the responsibility of the continuity manager.

The reconstitution manager cannot report that reconstitution is complete until the alternate facility has been restored to full readiness capability. This should be an item on the milestone checklist.

Reconstitution Element: Regions

For organizations with regional or field offices, coordination should be included in reconstitution planning. You will need to identify:

- Any issues that may need to be addressed.
- Any different issues if the devolution team is coordinating reconstitution.

This may be largely a communications matter, though in some situations, some organizational functions may have been transferred to regional offices. The question is, will these functions now stay with the region or be transferred back to HQ?

Note: The issue of regional facilities (which may be applicable at the State and local level as well) may not be a simple matter and should be carefully considered by all organizations. Determine what role regional offices will play!

Reconstitution Element: Regions

For organizations with regional or field offices, coordination should be included in reconstitution planning. You will need to identify:

- Any issues that may need to be addressed.
- Any different issues if the devolution team is coordinating reconstitution.

This may be largely a communications matter, though in some situations, some organizational functions may have been transferred to regional offices. The question is, will these functions now stay with the region or be transferred back to HQ?

Note: The issue of regional facilities (which may be applicable at the State and local level as well) may not be a simple matter and should be carefully considered by all organizations. Detemine what role will regional offices play!

Reconstitution Element: AAR

As the reconstitution effort proceeds, lessons learned should be captured in an after action report (AAR) by identifying:

- What was done well (i.e., best practices).
- What could have been done better (i.e., areas for improvement).
- What still needs to be addressed.

Lessons learned should also be recorded in the following:

- CAPs
- Improvement plans (IP)

Looking Ahead

Once reconstitution has been achieved, the (planning) process starts all over again.

Based on the experience gained, the continuity and reconstitution training program(s) can be modified to include the valuable lessons learned (both best practices and areas for improvement). These lessons should be shared with the organization and with partners.

Other improvements should be made, as appropriate, including identifying what can be done now to avoid unnecessary problems and complications in the future.

Summary

This concludes the lesson on elements of reconstitution. You should now be able to do the following:

- Identify the major elements of a comprehensive reconstitution plan.
- Describe the requirements for each element of the plan.

In lesson 6, you will learn about building a reconstitution plan.

Lesson 6 — Building a Reconstitution Plan

Overview

In this lesson, we will focus on organizing and outlining a (pre-event) reconstitution plan based on the reconstitution elements identified in Lesson 5. Individual organizations will most likely also want to address other issues and include materials and information unique to their organization.

Lesson Objectives

At the completion of this lesson, students will be able to do the following:

- Identify the major sections of a reconstitution plan.
- Describe the content that belongs in each section of a reconstitution plan.

FEMA Reconstitution Template

The FEMA reconstitution plan template is available for organizations to use as a guide for reconstitution plan development. It can, and should, be modified to meet individual organizational needs.

Remember, the purpose of the reconstitution plan is to provide organizational guidance and direction for resumption of full operations following a continuity crisis or disruption. The template includes information on authorities, concept of operations, implementation, and resource requirements, as well as checklists and appendices.

The template is just a starting point and addresses many of the issues that will need to be considered, but it is not a complete reconstitution plan. Organizations are not required to use the FEMA template. It is provided as a convenience. Alternate approaches are acceptable. However, while organizations are not required to use the template, Federal departments and agencies are required to have a reconstitution plan.

Note: For large organizations with a separate reconstitution team and complex reconstitution requirements, it may make sense to have a separate, stand-alone plan (that references information in the continuity plan). For small organizations, it may make more sense to include reconstitution as an annex to the continuity plan.

Developing the Reconstitution Plan

Organizations must identify and outline a plan to return to normal operations following a disruption, once leadership has determined that reconstitution operations for resuming normal business can be initiated. The plan must:

- Be executable and flexible (to accommodate a variety of situations).
- Include coordination and pre-planned options for reconstitution, while maintaining continuous support for essential functions.
- Identify records requirements for reconstitution (to include blueprints, communications/IT schematics, etc.).
- Address both short-term and long-term planning to include GSA, OPM, and NARA coordination requirements, as appropriate.

The reconstitution plan will also need to include update and maintenance requirements for the plan itself, as well as requirements for regular TT&E. There is continuous turnover of personnel, new hires, transfers, and reorganizations. Therefore, personnel will regularly need to review and be trained in the elements of even a well-written plan.

Reconstitution Plan Overview

The next two screens will provide a brief description of the specific sections in the reconstitution plan template:

- **Executive Summary** — Overview that provides the big picture and summary information.
- **Chapter 1, Introduction** — Describes the plan purpose, applicability and scope, types of reconstitution, plan objectives, planning assumptions, and responsibilities.
- **Chapter 2, Planning** — Outlines the planning aspects of reconstitution, including both pre-event planning and post-event planning. This chapter can also introduce reconstitution terminology, concepts, and challenges.
- **Chapter 3, Reconstitution Implementation** — Describes the processes, procedures, activities, and actions associated with implementing reconstitution.

Review the reconstitution plan template.

Reconstitution Plan Overview (continued)

- **Chapter 4, Reconstitution Training and Plan Management** — Describes responsibilities for managing and maintaining the plan, including training and exercises.

- **Appendices** — The appendices should include checklists, milestones, and other lists and guidance that will support the plan. It should be possible to modify appendices without going through a complex approval process.
- **Attachments** — There may be the data that fills in many of the plan details, but that will need to be regularly updated, such as lists of people, equipment, and records.

Keep in mind the differences between the following:

- Plan (which should receive formal approval by senior leadership and should not change frequently)
- Appendices (which may require approval at some level, but should be less complicated to modify)
- Attachments (which will be expected to change regularly)

Review the reconstitution plan template.

Executive Summary

The executive summary provides, in a few pages, a brief overview of the reconstitution plan and its most important elements — the big picture!

Though designed for senior executives, this overview may be all that most employees actually read. Therefore, it is worthwhile to make sure the executive summary presents a complete, though brief, overview of the plan, with links to where additional information can be found.

This section may be best written after the overall plan has been constructed.

Note: An additional option that departments and agencies may wish to consider is using a separate, brief handout (tri-fold type flyer) that addresses the overall plan for general distribution, supplemented by information prepared by individual components regarding their particular reconstitution issues and procedures.

Review the reconstitution plan template.

Chapter 1 — Introduction

Chapter 1 of the reconstitution plan should address the administrative aspects of the plan, including:

- Purpose

- Applicability and scope
- Plan organization
- Objectives
- Planning assumptions
- Authorities
- References
- Responsibilities (TT&E)
- Approval authority

The topics presented here are typical in many executive branch plans. The important issue is to include those areas required by the agency.

Review the reconstitution plan template.

Approval of the Plan

The approval authority and process should be delineated along with the administrative elements in Chapter 1. This could be included in the authorities section, or under its own section.

It is important to have the reconstitution plan approved (and endorsed) by senior leadership since it impacts and potentially affects every element of the organization. To ensure full participation and to make the plan effective, support from senior leadership is critical.

There is considerable value in getting each major organizational element to "sign off" on the plan. This brings more attention to the plan and demonstrates broad support for its requirements. This will likely be time-consuming, but will pay dividends in the long run. It will be hard for individual offices to resist doing their part if their leadership has endorsed the plan and its requirements.

Review the reconstitution plan template.

Chapter 2 — Planning

Chapter 2 identifies the various reconstitution planning teams, their members (by position or organization), and their responsibilities. The names of specific team members (and their backups) should be included in an attachment that can easily be modified and kept up to date. Also, it may be worthwhile to include the various associate planning team positions — contacts who may become involved only under certain circumstances.

Chapter 2 also provides an overview of the different phases of the reconstitution process, and the basic requirements and expectations for each phase. This can be referred to as the **concept of operations**.

Do not forget to include reconstitution by the devolution team as an element in this chapter.

Review the reconstitution plan template.

Concept of Operations

The phases of reconstitution include:

- Pre-event planning
- Post-event planning
- Implementation and reconstitution operations
- Reconstitution completion and post-reconstitution activities

Phases and Types of Reconstitution

For some organizations, a different approach may be required for the different types of reconstitution:

- **Primary facilities** — Going back to the original (repaired) primary facility.
- **Temporary facilities** — Moving to temporary facilities until repairs can be made or new permanent facilities are ready (note that "temporary" could mean several years).
- **New facilities** — Moving directly into a new permanent facility or facilities.

It may be appropriate to develop a matrix to address the possibilities and functions in each phase of reconstitution as a function of the type of reconstitution that may occur. An example is provided on the next screen.

Phases and Types of Reconstitution (continued)

This table outlines typical activities during each of the four phases of reconstitution (listed vertically on the left) for each of the three types of reconstitution (listed horizontally along the top). The focus is primarily on facility-related activities.

	Primary Facilities	Temporary Facilities	New Facilities
Pre-Event Planning	Write plans and TT&E	Write plans and TT&E	Write plans and TT&E
Post-Event Planning	Repairs to damaged facilities	Arrange space acquiring resources	Design space acquiring resources
Implementation	Coordinate orderly return	Coordinate transition	Coordinate transition
Reconstitution Completion Activities	Hot wash AAR	Hot wash AAR	Hot wash AAR

Note: The major elements that comprise pre-event planning and post-reconstitution activities will be largely the same. However, the post-event planning and implementation will have to be tailored to the type of reconstitution. These differences will have to be detailed in the reconstitution plan. This is a simple table. A more detailed table that includes issues of staff, records, security, and other issues may be a useful graphic to include in an agency reconstitution plan.

Pre-Event Planning

As previously discussed, the pre-event reconstitution planning will have to be general and include options to address a variety of possible disruptions and severities. Pre-event planning includes:

- Identifying planning team members
- Identifying reconstitution requirements
- Developing an executable reconstitution plan
- Gathering necessary supporting reference materials
- Obtaining organizational agreement with the plan
- Getting leadership approval of the plan
- Developing and conducting periodic training
- Testing and exercising the plan
- Maintaining, updating, and improving the plan

Post-Event Planning

It is important to recognize that planning refinement will continue throughout the entire reconstitution effort. Plans will frequently need to be updated and modified as they are implemented. Post-event planning includes:

- Assessing the actual (post-event) situation
- Identifying specific reconstitution requirements
- Establishing a detailed operational plan, including refining milestones
- Identifying individuals and organizations responsible for implementing each aspect of the plan
- Obtaining leadership approval of the operational plan
- Communicating the plan
- Monitoring progress and adjusting the plan and milestones as appropriate

Remember, the finalized post-event reconstitution plan will need to be approved. The process to do this should be addressed and outlined in the general plan.

Implementation

A detailed implementation plan will go a long way towards ensuring a smooth transition process. Implementation will involve actually following the plan, including:

- Organizing and monitoring repairs to facilities as needed
- Arranging temporary facilities
- Hiring personnel and/or contractors
- Training and certifying personnel (or new personnel)
- Purchasing replacement equipment
- Communicating with various groups
- Coordinating among organizational elements
- Tracking the status of missions and functions
- Verifying systems are operational

Implementation (continued)

Remember, MEFs and ESAs will continue to be performed by the ERG. The reconstitution effort will be to "bring back" on line all of the other organizational functions and ultimately restore the organization to full capability in a sustainable manner (long term operations). In addition, the reconstitution team, along with leadership, will have to determine the right time to move the ERG and essential functions to the restored or new facilities.

Human Capital Surge

Agencies must identify a human capital liaison from the agency's human resources staff to work with the reconstitution manager. Issues that will need to be addressed upon resuming normal operations may include:

- Employee assistance programs
- Availability of mental health professionals and counselors
- Hiring strategies, including rehire of retired personnel
- Strategies for expedited processing of clearances
- Assistance with claims processing related to healthcare and survivor's benefits

There are many other items that can be added to this list. Agencies should be prepared to deal with an increase in HR related activities. Being prepared to care for increased personnel issues can make a big difference in how smoothly the reconstitution process proceeds.

Reconstitution Completion

The reconstitution plan should outline what the end state will require, including:

- All organizational functions that were deferred are back up and running.
- The essential functions have been transferred to the primary facilities (repaired, temporary, or new).
- Alternate facilities that were used during continuity operations have been restored to readiness capability.
- Continuity and reconstitution hot washes have been conducted, and AARs and improvement plans have been (or are being) prepared.

Each department and agency will have to consider what completing reconstitution will mean for its individual circumstances. Many items will be common to most departments and agencies, but some may be unique.

Post-Reconstitution Activities

Following full reconstitution of all organizational functions (i.e., restoring normalcy), a review of the process, including what worked well and what could have been done better, should be performed. Although the staff will want to get on with "more important" work, capturing lessons learned is an important step in not making the same mistakes again.

- Participants should be interviewed or asked to participate in a hot wash. This includes leadership.
- Input should be collected, documented, and added into lessons learned as part of an AAR that includes a CAP.

The CAP may include improvements to the continuity plan and the reconstitution plan. It may include items for various program offices to improve readiness. Note that the window to make improvements will likely be short-lived. The staff will be anxious to get back to work and move on.

The CAP should also identify individuals responsible for actions and timeframes by which they should be completed. This will need to be tracked and monitored or it may never get done.

Chapter 3 — Reconstitution Implementation

Implementation is the core of the reconstitution plan and should provide (or reference) details and checklists to facilitate getting the job done. Each element of the detailed implementation plan should identify or reference (as appropriate) the following:

- What needs to be accomplished
- Who is responsible for seeing that the work is completed
- What are the milestones and deadlines to complete the work
- What supplies, support, and financing will be needed and who is responsible for providing these
- What metrics will be used to determine when each item is complete

Review the reconstitution plan template.

Chapter 3 — Reconstitution Implementation (continued)

The individual(s) or organization(s) responsible for completing each portion of the work can be expected to obtain appropriate records and resources to get the work done, or to identify additional assistance that is needed. The bottom line is that clarity with regard to responsibilities is key.

Some "big picture" checklists and data may be included directly in Chapter 3. More detailed checklists and those that are more likely to change over time may be included as appendices or attachments so they can be modified without having to revise the entire plan.

Each subordinate organization will have to monitor its own reconstitution progress and follow the overall schedule established by the reconstitution team. Coordinating these efforts will be important to ensure smooth implementation and should be addressed. Planners should consider how to monitor the progress of each of the individual subordinate organizations.

Review the reconstitution plan template.

Chapter 3 — Reconstitution Implementation (continued)

This chapter outlines processes and procedures that include:

- Conducting assessments and salvaging, restoring, and/or recovering
- Conducting security, safety, and health assessments
- Reoccupying original, temporary, rebuilt, or new facilities
- Managing the return of personnel, equipment, and records
- Drawing down continuity or devolution operations
- Transferring essential functions, resuming all Government functions, and securing continuity operations (i.e., demobilizing)
- Identifying and recovering essential records and databases
- Periodically reporting operational status

Review the reconstitution plan template.

Chapter 3 — Reconstitution Implementation (continued)

Each of the topics (and others, as needed) mentioned on the previous screen should be addressed in this chapter, along with guidance and requirements. While many of the broad topics may be similar from one organization to the next, the details of implementing these areas are likely to vary considerably with the size, structure, location, and missions of different organizations. Make sure you include checklists for each major activity.

Review the reconstitution plan template.

Checklists for Each Element

For each reconstitution element discussed in Lesson 5, you should develop a checklist (or series of checklists) that outlines requirements should be developed. Tables such as this may provide a useful means to identify required actions and responsible organizations, as well as a means to monitor overall progress and identify obstacles.

	Primary Facilities	Temporary Facilities	New Facilities
Plans/Milestones			
Facilities			
People			
Comms/IT			
Messaging			
Records			
Functions			
Safety			
Security			

Once the actual situation is understood, a table such as this can be constructed to align with actual conditions and expectations. It may be more useful to use a larger database, such as an Excel spreadsheet, for the actual plan.

Determining Requirements

This screen presents an example of the kind of information that each organization may want to identify and document as part of its plan. To determine what information you need to identify and document, ask yourself questions such as:

- Has the organization developed a process for determining the degree of damage to the primary facility?
- Is there a list of all available facilities that the organization "owns" that could be used as temporary facilities?
- Has the organization identified critical factors that cannot be compromised in a temporary or new primary facility?

Resumption of Normal Operations

Remember, reconstitution includes the resumption of non-essential functions. These are questions that EVERY office or component of the organization needs to address as part of its portion of the overall reconstitution plan:

- Does every office have stored information on how day-to-day business is done?
- What if no one in that office survives? Can someone else figure out how to re-establish those operations?
- Who knows where the records back-up records and back-up records are stored, and how they are organized?
- Does someone know the personnel requirements and skill sets necessary to perform these functions?
- Who were the customers, partners, and stakeholders?

It may be appropriate to have every office create a reference list that addresses its processes and requirements to assist whomever must coordinate that office's reconstitution effort. These lists can be assembled as attachments to the plan.

Component Considerations

A key planning element is to identify and ensure the availability of the resources and capabilities needed to support all reconstitution operations. This includes resources such as people, equipment, furniture, and supplies and capabilities such as internet connectivity, communications, and information technology. Ensuring that these requirements can be met is key to the organization's ability to effectively transfer and continue performance of essential functions as well as resume all other Government functions. The specific requirements will depend on the type of reconstitution, but in general the requirements will be similar.

Once the organization has developed its overall reconstitution concept of operations and plan, it will be necessary for EVERY component within the organization to assess and document its specific requirements and needs. Some of this information (particularly for offices that provide support to the entire organization, such as IT, Security, and space management) will need to be incorporated into the overall plan. Other information may be included in attachments or maintained by the individual component.

Chapter 4 — Plan Maintenance and Training

To remain effective, the reconstitution plan will need to be reviewed and updated regularly. A schedule for reviewing each part of the plan should be developed and included as an appendix for personnel lists and contact information. Essential functions may only require annual review.

Regular TT&E will need to be planned, conducted, and documented!

This section should identify who is responsible for these actions.

Review the reconstitution plan template.

Reconstitution Training

Unlike continuity training, which focuses primarily on components with essential functions (MEFs and ESAs), reconstitution planning and training must involve every office in the organization.

Every new employee (including contractor staff) should receive some basic initial continuity and reconstitution training and periodic refresher training. This continuity and reconstitution training should be included with the basic orientation training for all employees, including the occupant emergency plan (OEP), safety, security, time and attendance, etc.

How will this training be accomplished in your organization? The objective is to create a culture in which continuity and reconstitution are included in everyone's job description. Once the broader community understands the concepts and goals of continuity, employees can conduct business in a "continuity-wise" manner. This is similar to the concept of conducting business in an "environmentally aware" manner.

Reconstitution Plan Appendices

The appendices provide additional information and detail to enhance and further support reconstitution plan implementation. Typically, the appendices will include non-policy information that may change periodically, or that may be primarily of interest to only a portion of the organization. Separating this information from the main plan will make it easier to modify and keep current. Some suggested appendices are listed below:

- Essential functions (can just be referenced)
- Organizational chart(s)
- Space requirements (including blueprints)

- IT schematics
- Reconstitution records
- Milestone template(s)
- AAR/IP template(s)
- Definitions and acronyms

Review the reconstitution plan template.

Reconstitution Plan Appendices (continued)

An organization may choose to have an appendix (or attachment) for forms. These forms can be included with specific subject matter topics. Forms of interest may include:

- Continuity status reporting (CSR) forms
- GSA Forms
- Internal agency forms

The reconstitution records appendix should include a records schedule to assist with the reconstitution of the complete set of agency records back to normal operations. An essential records packet can be used to reconstitute the emergency operating records and the rights and interest records that will be needed to prepare for the next continuity event. NARA can provide additional assistance with all records storage, maintenance, and recovery-related matters.

Review the reconstitution plan template.

Reconstitution Plan Attachments

The attachments provide additional information and detail to enhance and further support reconstitution plan implementation. Attachments may include:

- Checklists
- Point-of-contact lists
- Repair contractors
- Pre-staged public affairs and communications statements

Review the reconstitution plan template.

Chapter 5 — Field and Regional Responsibilities

Reconstitution needs to be viewed from a broad perspective, involving the entire organization, not just headquarters or one office. Keeping this in mind, you may need to include an additional chapter (call it Chapter 5 — Field and Regional Responsibilities) in your reconstitution plan that incorporates consideration of field and regional activities, since some functions may be temporarily reconstituted at a regional office, or even transferred there permanently.

Some functions may involve critical input or actions by regional offices. These offices will need to understand the organization's plans and expectations so they are fully prepared and integrated into continuity and reconstitution activities.

Representation from regional offices should be included in all aspects of reconstitution planning (including training), both from the perspective of how they will support a headquarters continuity and reconstitution effort AND how they will plan and implement their own continuity and reconstitution programs if that becomes necessary.

Reconstitution of Departmental or Regional Facilities

Organizations should consider reconstitution planning in all locations, not just those that support MEFs. Organizational functions (not just MEFs) are often performed in locations other than the headquarters, such as regional facilities. The activities at regional facilities need both continuity and reconstitution plans.

Incorporating regional activities in the planning process may expand and complicate the effort, but it also involves portions of the organization that may need to be included in both planning and implementation. Equally important is the consideration that a disruptive event may be just as likely at a regional office as at headquarters. Can the organization continue operations if regional activities shut down? How quickly does the regional office need to restore operations?

Reconstitution for Devolution Plans — Special Considerations

The reconstitution manager role and membership of the reconstitution planning team must be replicated and training must be implemented for the devolution team. In addition, the reconstitution plan should work for both the ERG and the devolution emergency response group (DERG) teams.

Reconstitution by the devolution team has special considerations that must be addressed. For example, the DERG team may not be particularly familiar with the headquarters region, and planning will be needed for personnel accountability in an area that is geographically removed.

How the devolution team will address reconstitution will vary considerably from organization to organization. This is an issue the reconstitution team should address with their devolution team counterparts. For example, the DERG needs to know to keep the CRC informed.

Summary

This concludes the lesson on elements of reconstitution. You should now be able to do the following:

- Identify the major sections of a reconstitution plan.
- Describe the content that belongs in each section of a reconstitution plan.

In lesson 7, you will review a summary of the content in this course.

Lesson 7 — Course Summary

Overview

This lesson provides a brief summary of the Reconstitution Planning course.

Reconstitution

Reconstitution is one of the 10 elements of continuity. In addition, reconstitution:

- Is an essential function.
- Requires a plan and essential records.
- Involves essential personnel — the ERG team.
- Requires TT&E.

Keep in mind, continuity is focused on the most important and urgent functions, whereas reconstitution concerns EVERYTHING!

Additionally, only a select few people are directly involved in continuity operations (the ERG), whereas reconstitution planning involves everyone in the organization.

Scope of Reconstitution

Reconstitution can be as **simple** as offices being fully open following limited operations after a snowstorm and all employees expected to report to work for normal operations. Another example would be if an office had a fire and employees were informed they could return to work.

OR

Reconstitution can be as **complicated** as recovering from an attack such as the one on the World Trade Center, with challenges that include relocation of operations with survivors — first to a temporary location for full operations, and then to a new permanent location.

Reconstitution, as well as continuity, are ultimately about performing **FUNCTIONS**.

Reconstitution Planning

Reconstitution planning begins **now** as an element of a comprehensive continuity planning process.

The reconstitution manager should **not** be the continuity manager (if possible). Many organizations use a key staff member from facilities management, logistics, security, or similar functions to lead the reconstitution team.

Reconstitution activities should start very shortly after the activation of the continuity plan in order to begin consideration of the return to full and normal operations as quickly as possible.

Note: The reconstitution planning manager may or may not be the same person as the reconstitution implementation manager.

Lesson 2: Reconstitution Requirements

In lesson 2, you learned how to:

- Describe the role of reconstitution in overall continuity.
- Identify reconstitution plan requirements.
- Identify reconstitution implementation requirements.

Lesson 3: Types of Reconstitution

In lesson 3, you learned how to:

- Describe when reconstitution may be required.
- Identify different types of reconstitution.
- Identify the four different phases of reconstitution.
- Identify the difference between pre-event and post-event reconstitution planning.

Lesson 4: Reconstitution Teams

In lesson 4, you learned how to:

- Identify the responsibilities of the reconstitution manager.
- Identify who should be on the reconstitution planning team.
- Identify the goals of the reconstitution planning team.
- Identify who should be on the reconstitution implementation team.
- Identify the work that must be conducted by the reconstitution implementation team.

Lesson 5: Elements of Reconstitution

In lesson 5, you learned how to:

- Identify the major elements of a comprehensive reconstitution plan.
- Describe the requirements for each element of the plan.
- Identify any additional reconstitution elements.

Lesson 5: Elements of Reconstitution

In lesson 5, you learned how to:

- Identify the major elements of a comprehensive reconstitution plan.
- Describe the requirements for each element of the plan.
- Identify any additional reconstitution elements.

Lesson 6: Building a Reconstitution Plan

In lesson 6, you learned how to:

- Outline the major sections of a reconstitution plan.
- Describe the content that belongs in each section of a reconstitution plan.

Conclusion

This concludes the Reconstitution Planning course.

Remember to identify and explore the requirements and information indentified in this course needed to build and execute a comprehensive reconstitution plan that will meet the needs of your organization.

Congratulations and good luck!